I will, with God's help

T0273389

Mentor's Guide

by LINDA NICHOLS

Morehouse Education Resources
a division of Church Publishing Incorporated
600 Grant Street, Suite 630
Denver, CO 80203

Morehouse Eduction Resources
        a division of Church Publishing Incorporated

Editorial Offices:
600 Grant Street, Suite 630
Denver, CO 80203

Cover Design: Jim Lemons
Cover Photograph: Regan MacStravic
Page Design: Vicky Rees
Editing: Mary Lee Wile

Printed in the United States of America.

The scripture quotations used herein are from the New Revised Standard Version Bible. © 1989 by the Division of Christian Education of the National Council of Churches of Christ.

Excerpts from The Book of Common Prayer and Administration of the Sacraments and Other Rites and Ceremonies of the Church, published by Church Publishing Corporation, 1979.

ISBN 978-1-60674-056-9

Table of Contents

Introduction

Dear Mentor,

The mentoring process deepens confirmation preparation. Mentoring provides an opportunity for invaluable one-on-one time with a confirmation student. Mentors serve as companions to help confirmands examine their faith at this point in their journey, wherever they might be.

This book is written with no right or wrong answers; it is designed simply to help you explore the Baptismal Covenant. Questions are open-ended to assist in quality conversation about what we read in scripture and how we can respond in our daily lives to the call of Christ.

In the Episcopal tradition, we have a three-year lectionary in which there is a primary gospel for our worship readings: Year A is Matthew, Year B is Mark and Year C is Luke. This book is designed to use the gospel appointed for this year (and/or the gospel that speaks to you). Plan to meet with your student between six and eight times. It will be helpful for each of you to have both a Bible and a *Book of Common Prayer*. Read together and discuss what touches each of you the most. As a mentor, your task is to listen carefully to this young person and affirm both the struggles and triumphs that he or she experiences.

This *Mentor's Guide*, inspired by *I will, with God's Help* by Mary Lee Wile, was designed as a supplement to this resource. I offer special thanks to those in the field who have already found the *Mentor's Guide* helpful and worthy to share with others. It is my prayerful hope for all students to reaffirm their Baptismal vows the day of Confirmation with a full understanding of what is being asked of them. These questions from the Baptismal Covenant frame our liturgy of both Baptism and Confirmation, and the most appropriate response is "*I will, with God's help*," for it is with God's help that we have arrived at this place. Peace to you for your journey toward that understanding.

In Christ,
Linda

Linda W. Nichols
Christian Educator

Session 1: I Believe

PLAN THE SESSION

Celebrant: Do you believe in God the Father?

People: I believe in God, the Father almighty, creator of heaven and earth.

Celebrant: Do you believe in Jesus Christ, the Son of God?

People: I believe in Jesus Christ, his holy Son, our Lord.

He was conceived by the power of the Holy Spirit and born of the Virgin Mary.

He suffered under Pontius Pilate, was crucified, died, and was buried.

He descended to the dead.

On the third day he rose again.

He ascended into heaven, and is seated at the right hand of the Father.

He will come again to judge the living and the dead.

Celebrant: *Do you believe in God the Holy Spirit?*
People: *I believe in the Holy Spirit,*
  the holy catholic church,
  the forgiveness of sins,
  the resurrection of the body,
  and the life everlasting.

Celebrant: *Will you continue in the apostles' teaching and*
  fellowship, in the breaking of bread, and in the prayers?
People: *I will, with God's help.*

Celebrant: *Will you persevere in resisting evil, and whenever you*
  fall into sin, repent and return to the Lord?
People: *I will, with God's help.*

Celebrant: *Will you proclaim by word and example the Good News*
  of God in Christ?
People: *I will, with God's help.*

Celebrant: *Will you seek and serve Christ in all persons, loving*
  your neighbor as yourself?
People: *I will, with God's help.*

Celebrant: *Will you strive for justice and peace among all people,*
  and respect the dignity of every human being?
People: *I will, with God's help.*

To Bring

- 2 Bibles
- 2 copies of *The Book of Common Prayer*

Matters of Time and Place

How much time you spend on each session can be flexible, depending on what you and the confirmand you will be mentoring have available, but aim for between 45 minutes and an hour and a half. Choose a meeting place that will be comfortable for both of you: a quiet room at church, the student's home, your home, a coffee shop or even somewhere outside if weather permits.

The Session at a Glance

- Welcome the student you will be mentoring.
- Get better acquainted.
- Pray the Baptismal Covenant responsively and offer background on the Creed.
- Share questions and conversation.
- Close with prayer.

Before the Session

- Select a meeting place.
- Extend a personal invitation to the confirmand you will be mentoring, either in person or by telephone.
- Have two copies of *The Book of Common Prayer* and two Bibles in hand.
- Read through the background information on the Apostles' Creed (p. 12), the suggested scripture passages, and the questions for conversation. Note your own responses to the questions.

THE SESSION

Gather

Welcome the student you are accompanying as mentor on his or her journey of faith. If you do not know each other well, consider spending time getting acquainted by sharing such things as background and interests, talents and passions.

To initiate the Session, turn to page 304 in *The Book of Common Prayer* and pray the whole Baptismal Covenant, with the student as *Celebrant* and you as *People*.

This would be a good place to share some (or all) of the background information about the Apostles' Creed, on which the opening three questions of the Baptismal Covenant are based.

For each of the following "Focus" segments, read the selected scripture passages and consider the questions for conversation.

Focus: Communion of Saints and the Communal Nature of the Creeds

Discuss:
- What does it mean to be connected to those who lived before and after us and universally?
- The Rev. Barbara Brown Taylor (p. 71) says "When I say, 'We believe...' I count on that to cover what I cannot believe on my own right now. When my faith limps, I lean on the faith of the church, letting 'our' faith suffice until mine returns. Later, when I am able to say, 'We believe...' with

renewed confidence, I know that I am filling in for others who are indisposed for the time being, as they filled in for me. My decision to say the creed at all is a decision to trust those who have gone before me, embracing the faith they have commended to me."

- "We" vs. "I" believe; can you name an occasion when you've stood as an individual in companionship/unity with others? Do you feel most comfortable speaking as an individual in a group or in the unity of one collective group? See *The Book of Common Prayer (BCP)*, pages 326-8 where there is an option of using the plural vs. individual form of the Nicene Creed.
- What does *God, One in Three, Three in One*, encompass for you?

Focus: "Creed" as One's Deepest Belief

Discuss:

- Is there anything you believe in so much you would be willing to shout it in front of a crowded room?
- In the Gospel of Luke, there are statements of conviction that have been incorporated into our liturgies of Morning and Evening Prayer, called Canticles.

Read and discuss the following. Which passages do you like and why?

- Song of Mary/The Magnificat—Luke 1:46-55—BCP pages 91 (Canticle 15) and 119
- Zechariah's Prophecy—Luke 1:67-79—BCP page 92 (Canticle 16)
- Angel's Announcement/Gloria—Luke 2:14—BCP page 94 (Canticle 20)

- Simeon's Proclamation—Luke 2:29-32—BCP page 93 (Canticle 17)
- John the Baptist—Luke 3:4-6
- Jesus' Mission—Luke 4:16-19
- Declaration of Peter—Luke 9:18-20

Closing

Close your time together by praying the Lord's Prayer and/or the following selected stanzas from St. Patrick's Breastplate (*The Hymnal 1982*, #370):

> *I bind unto myself today*
> *The strong name of the Trinity,*
> *By invocation of the same,*
> *The Three in One and One in Three.*
> *Christ be with me, Christ within me,*
> *Christ behind me, Christ before me,*
> *Christ beside me, Christ to win me,*
> *Christ to comfort and restore me,*
> *Christ beneath me, Christ above me,*
> *Christ in quiet, Christ in danger,*
> *Christ in hearts of all that love me,*
> *Christ in mouth of friend and stranger.*

BACKGROUND ON
THE APOSTLES' CREED

The first three questions of the Baptismal Covenant comprise the Apostle's Creed, which, as our oldest creed, has stood the test of time. Legend has it that this creed was written by the apostles of Jesus before they left Jerusalem to go spread the Good News to all corners of the earth. The truth is that the source remains unknown, but it does in fact predate all other Christian creeds, including the Nicene Creed, which was drafted during the Council of Nicaea in 325 A.D. and completed at the next council (at Constantinople in 381 A.D.); the Nicene Creed was designed to set the boundaries of orthodox doctrine, standardizing the Christian set of beliefs (Young pp. 2-4). Each generation continues to examine their beliefs in the context of the creeds as an intricate part of both tradition and liturgy of the Church.

Creeds are declarations and summaries of the faith. In the early Church, creeds were used to teach the faith and to baptize new believers. At Baptism, a priest would ask the first question, the candidates for Baptism would answer it, and the priest would then baptize them in the name of God the Father. The priest proceeded to ask a second question, which the candidates again answered, after which they were baptized in the name of Jesus Christ. After the third question and answer, the priest then baptized them in the name of the Holy Spirit. Their answers provided a statement of faith, an understanding of the Trinity (Young, pp. 6-9). Past and present, around the world, down through all the ages, Christians are baptized with this Trinitarian formula: *in the Name of the Father, and of the Son, and of the Holy Spirit.*

Since most first century folks did not read or write, the oral question and answer format became the established method of catechizing or "teaching" the summaries of the faith and gospels. We have records dating back to Hippolytus c.200 A.D. that attest to a question and answer process in the liturgy of Baptism. This format continued throughout the centuries as the primary process for catechism, or instruction in the Faith (see "An Outline of the Faith: commonly called the Catechism" in *The Book of Common Prayer*, pp. 843-62).

Jesus often asked questions as a means of entering into a teachable moment. "Who do you say that I am?" Take a moment to look up Peter's response to this question in Luke 9:18-20. Another time, Jesus asked, "Do you believe in the Son of Man?" "I believe, Lord," was the response of the healed beggar in John 9:35, 38. Thus, "I believe" continues to be the proclamation of personal belief.

God's love created the world; God's love became incarnate in Christ Jesus so love could dwell among us and be our example and God's love continues in the Holy Spirit to guide us today. The Apostles' Creed is the backbone of the Baptismal Covenant; the 1979 *Book of Common Prayer* restored the Creed to the question and answer format in both our Baptism and Confirmation liturgies.

Session 2: Teaching and Fellowship, Bread and Prayers

PLAN THE SESSION

Celebrant: Will you continue in the apostles'
teaching and fellowship, in the breaking
of bread, and in the prayers?

People: I will, with God's help.

To Bring

- 2 Bibles
- 2 copies of *The Book of Common Prayer*

Optional:
- Anglican prayer beads
- bread (or other baked goods) to share

Matters of Time and Place

How much time you spend on each Session can be
flexible, depending on what you and the confirmand you
are mentoring have available, but aim for between 45
minutes and an hour and a half.

This second session covers a wealth of scripture readings and includes a variety of questions which may extend your conversation (although quieter students may be done sooner—hence the need for flexibility).

Choose a meeting place that will be comfortable for both of you: a quiet room at church, the student's home, your home, a coffee shop, or even somewhere outside if weather permits.

The Session at a Glance

- Welcome the student you are mentoring; do a check-in to see how you both have been faring since your previous Session.
- Pray the appropriate vow from the Baptismal Covenant responsively.
- *Optional: share bread or other baked goods.*
- Share questions and conversation.
- *Optional: explore the use of Anglican prayer beads.*
- Close with prayer.

Before the Session

- Select a meeting place.
- Extend an e-mail or phone invitation to the confirmand you are mentoring.
- Have two copies of *The Book of Common Prayer* and two Bibles in hand, and (if desired) the bread and beads.
- Read through the suggested scripture passages and the questions for conversation. Note your own responses to the questions.

THE SESSION

Gather

Welcome the student you are accompanying as mentor on his or her journey of faith. Take time to check in with each other about any important events, experiences or ideas you have each encountered since you last met.

To initiate the Session, turn to page 304 in *The Book of Common Prayer* and pray the appropriate vow from the Baptismal Covenant together, with the student as *Celebrant* and you as *People*.

Optional: Share the bread or baked goods; talk about table fellowship, shared meals, favorite memories of food, etc.

For each of the following "Focus" segments, read the selected scripture passages and consider the questions for conversation.

Focus: Teaching—What Are the "Teachings" of the Kingdom?

Year A—*Matthew*
- Beatitudes—Matthew 5:3-11
- Golden Rule—Matthew 7:12
- Parables—Sower: Matthew 13:1-9; Banquet: Matthew 22:1-14
- Healings—Leper: Matthew 8:1-4; Demons: Matthew 8:28-34

Year B—*Mark*
- Parables—Sower: Mark 4:1-12; Banquet: Luke 14:15-24
- Healings—Leper: Mark 1:40-45; Demons: Mark 5:1-20

Year C—Luke
- Parables—Sower: Luke 8:4-15; Banquet: Luke 14:15-24
- Healings—Paralytic: Luke 5:12-26; Demons: Luke 8:26-39

Discuss:
- What do you think is essential to pass down to the next generation?

Focus: Fellowship

- Jesus as a Boy Stayed Behind in the Temple— Luke 2:41-52

Discuss:
- Do you feel at home in church? Why or why not?
- Where do we find community in our lives?

Focus: Breaking of Bread—Last Supper and Post Resurrection

Year A—Matthew
- Matthew 26:26-30
- Matthew 28:5-20

Year B—Mark
- Mark 14:22-26
- Mark 16:1-20

Year C—Luke
- Luke 22:7-30
- Luke 24:13-49

Discuss:
- Where does the Eucharist come from?
- How is Christ revealed today?

Focus: Prayers

Year A—Matthew
- Come to Me: Matthew 11:25-30
- The Lord's Prayer: Matthew 6:5-15

Year B—Mark
- Garden of Gethsemane (Thy will be done): Mark 14:32-42

Year C—Luke
- The Lord's Prayer: Luke 11:1-23

Discuss:
- *The Book of Common Prayer* has two versions of the Lord's Prayer. With which do you feel most comfortable? (See pp. 97, 121 or 364.)
- Why is a "formula" like the Lord's Prayer a perfect example of prayer?
- Is there a prayer that has special meaning for you?

Optional: All world religions have prayer beads as aids to help us in prayer. Many find solace in the Anglican prayer beads. You may want to explore this avenue of prayer.

Closing

Close by saying the Lord's Prayer together. If you have spent time with the Anglican prayer beads, you might consider praying with them.

Session 3: Resist, Repent and Return

PLAN THE SESSION

Celebrant: *Will you persevere in resisting evil, and*
whenever you fall into sin, repent and
return to the Lord?

People: *I will, with God's help.*

To Bring

- 2 Bibles
- 2 copies of *The Book of Common Prayer*

Matters of Time and Place

How much time you spend on each Session can be
flexible, depending on what you and the confirmand you
are mentoring have available, but aim for between 45
minutes and an hour and a half.

Because this third Session focuses
on sin and repentance, you might
want to select a meeting place that
will have a measure of privacy for both of you: a quiet
room at church, the student's home, your home, or even
somewhere outside if weather permits. This probably
is not a time to meet in a public place such as a coffee
shop.

The Session at a Glance

- Welcome the student you are mentoring; do a check-in to see how you both have been faring since your previous Session.
- Pray the appropriate vow from the Baptismal Covenant responsively.
- Share questions and conversation.
- Close with prayer.

Before the Session

- Select a meeting place.
- Extend an e-mail or phone invitation to the confirmand you're mentoring.
- Have two copies of *The Book of Common Prayer* and two Bibles in hand.
- Read through the suggested scripture passages and the questions for conversation; note your own responses to the questions.

THE SESSION

Gather

Welcome the student you are accompanying as mentor on his or her journey of faith. Take time to check in with each other about any important events, experiences or ideas you have encountered since you last met.

To initiate the session, turn to page 304 in *The Book of Common Prayer* and pray the appropriate vow from the Baptismal Covenant, with the student as *Celebrant* and you as *People*.

For each of the following "Focus" segments, read the selected scripture passages and consider the questions for conversation.

Focus: To Resist—Jesus' Temptation

Year A—Matthew
• Matthew 4:1-11

Year B—Mark
• Mark 1:9-13

Year C—Luke
• Luke 4:1-13

Discuss:
• Jesus was tempted too! Can you recall a time when someone dared you to do something?
• Did you take the dare or not? Why or why not?
• What could someone tempt you with that you couldn't refuse? Why?

Focus: To Resist—Jesus' Parables

Year A—Matthew
• Parable of the the Rich Man— Luke 12:13-21
• The Narrow Door—Matthew 7:13-14, Matthew 7:21-23
• The Lost Sheep—Matthew 18:10-20

Year B—Mark
- Parable of the Rich Man—Mark 10:17-31
- Outcasts/Levi—Mark 2:13-17
- Children—Mark 9:33-37

Year C—Luke
- Parable of the Rich Man—Luke 12:13-21
- The Narrow Door—Luke13:22-30
- The Prodigal Son—Luke 15:11-32
- The Lost Sheep—Luke 15:1-10

Discuss:
- Who will be saved? Do you believe everyone will go to heaven?

Focus: To Repent—Forgiveness

Year A—Matthew
- Turn from Sin—Luke 13:1-5
- The Millstone—Matthew 18:6-9
- The Unforgiving Servant—Matthew 18:21-35

Year B—Mark
- Turn from Sin—Luke 13:1-5
- The Millstone—Mark 9:42-50
- The Paralyzed Man—Mark 2:1-12
- Peter's Denial—Mark 14:27-31

Year C—Luke
- Turn from Sin—Luke 13:1-5
- The Women with the Aabaster Jar—Luke 7:36-50
- The Millstone—Luke 17:1-6

Discuss:
- The moments we know that God is working in our lives are when:
  — we need to make difficult decisions
  — we don't always do what we want but what is good for others
  — we resist the temptation to do something we know to be wrong
  — we help our friends and even those who are not our friends
  — we say, "I'm sorry" and mean it
  — we accept someone's apology
- Do you think someone can be forgiven without repenting?
- How have you sought God's help?

Jesus Prayer—Luke 18:13 (9-14); Luke 18:38 (35-43):
- O (Lord) God, have mercy on me (a sinner). *Amen.*

Discuss:
- How does prayer sustain us through mistakes?

Jesus Died to Sin and Death—Luke 23:26-49
- How does this sacrifice made on our behalf make us stronger to resist evil?
- Do we really believe Christ died for our sins once and for all?
- Why do we act like orphans instead of children of the King?

Good vs. Evil (Parable of Tenants in the Vineyard)— Luke 20:9-19
- How does Jesus make a difference in the fight of good over evil?

Focus: To Return

Today you may have read passages from Luke: the
Prodigal Son (Luke 15:11-32) and the Lost Sheep
(Luke 15:1-10). Jesus came to find the "lost." God does
not play Hide and Seek, although we are free to walk
away at any time and to return as did the Prodigal Son.
God will always take us back, no matter how long or
how far we have strayed. However, part of returning is
acknowledging our actions and asking God to help us
find recompense/atonement for our past. The first step
is a contrite heart.

Closing

Close by saying the Lord's Prayer together or another
favorite prayer.

You might also select one of the prayers of confession
from *The Book of Common Prayer*, such as the one on
page 41, the "Penitential Order" (pp. 351-53), the
"Litany of Penitence" (pp. 267-69), or Form Two of
the "Reconciliation of a Penitent" (pp. 449-452) which
references the Parable of the Prodigal Son, or the more
familiar confession on page 360.

Close with the reminder that God always desires to
forgive us and help us.

Session 4: Word and Example

PLAN THE SESSION

Celebrant: *Will you proclaim by word and example the Good News of God in Christ?*

People: *I will, with God's help.*

To Bring

- 2 Bibles
- 2 copies of *The Book of Common Prayer*

Matters of Time and Place

How much time you spend on each session can be flexible, depending on what you and the confirmand you will be mentoring have available, but aim for between 45 minutes and an hour and a half. Choose a meeting place that will be comfortable for both of you: a quiet room at church, the student's home, your home, a coffee shop or even somewhere outside if weather permits.

The Session at a Glance

- Welcome the student you are mentoring. Do a check-in to see how you both have been faring since your previous session.
- Pray the appropriate vow from the Baptismal Covenant responsively.
- Share questions and conversation.
- Close with prayer.

Before the Session

- Select a meeting place.
- Extend an e-mail or phone invitation to the confirmand you're mentoring.
- Have two copies of *The Book of Common Prayer* and two Bibles in hand.
- Read through the suggested scripture passages and the questions for conversation. Note your own responses to the questions.

THE SESSION

Gather

Welcome the student you are accompanying as mentor on his or her journey of faith. Take time to check in with each other about any important events, experiences or ideas you have encountered since you last met.

To initiate this session, turn to page 305 in *The Book of Common Prayer* and pray the appropriate vow from the Baptismal Covenant, with the student as *Celebrant* and you as *People*.

For each of the following "Focus" segments, read the selected scripture passages and consider the questions for conversation.

Focus: Our "Call"

Year A—Matthew
• Matthew 28:1-10

Year B—Mark
• Mark 1:9-13

Year C—Luke
• Luke 24:1-11

Discuss:
• The resurrection is Good News. What makes it good?
• We are each called to "proclaim" the Good News, but first we must decide what it means for each of us. What is the Good News in your life?

Focus: The Word/Jesus' Call—Teaching Parables, Love, Calling the "Lost" to the Fold

Year A—Matthew
• Healing
    — Woman—Matthew 9:18-26
    — Blind Men—Matthew 9:27-31
    — The Beggar—Matthew 9:32-38
• Miracles
    — Calming of the Sea—Matthew 8:23-27
    — Feeding of the 5,000—Matthew 14:13-21
    — Walking on Water—Matthew 14:22-32

Year B—Mark
- Healing
  - — Woman—Mark 5:21-41
  - — Blind Men—Mark 10:46-52, Mark 8: 22-26
  - — Beelzebub—Mark 3:20-30
- Miracles
  - — Calming of the sea—Mark 4:35-41
  - — Feeding of the 5,000—Mark 6:30-44
  - — Walking on Water—Mark 6:45-52

Year C—Luke
- Healing
  - — Blind Man—Luke 18:35-43
  - — Woman—Luke 8:40-56
  - — Beggar—Luke 18:35-43
- Miracles
  - — Calming of the Sea—Luke 8:22-25
  - — Feeding of the 5,000—Luke 9:10-17

Discuss:
- Describe how Jesus continues to bring us/others closer to God.

Focus: By Word and Example

Year A—Matthew
- Lamp of the Body—Matthew 6:22-23:
  - — How is the eye the lamp of the body?
  - — How do we use eye contact to communicate?
  - — What happens when we look others in the eye?
- Judging Others—Matthew 7:1-6
- Bearing of Good Fruit—Matthew 7:15-20
- Salt and Light—Matthew 5:14-16
- Parable of Two Sons—Matthew 21:28-32
- Will You Follow?—Matthew 8:19-22

I will, with God's help

Year B—Mark

- Lamp of the Body—Luke 11:33-36:
  - — How is the eye the lamp of the body?
  - — How do we use eye contact to communicate?
  - — What happens when we look others in the eye?
- Lamp under a Bowl—Mark 4:21-25
- Faith—7:14-30
- The Hour—Mark 13:32-37
- Will You Follow?—Mark 8:31-37

Year C—Luke

- Lamp of the Body—Luke 11:33-36
  - — How is the eye the lamp of the body?
  - — How do we use eye contact to communicate?
  - — What happens when we look others in the eye?
- Bearing of Good Fruit—Luke 6:43-45
- Light under a Bowl—Luke 8:16-18
- Will You Follow?—Luke 9:57-62

How do our actions speak louder than words?
Do our words match our actions?

Focus: Response of Gratitude—Stewardship Is a Response of Thankfulness

Year A—Matthew

- Where is Your Heart?—Matthew 6:19-21, 24-34
- Parable of the Workers in the Vineyard— Matthew 20:1-16
- Parable of Hidden Treasure, Pearl and Net— Matthew 13:44-50

Year B—Mark
- Where Is Your Heart?—Luke 12:32-40
- Parable of Shrewd Manager—Luke 16:1-13
- Widow's Mite—Mark 12:41-44

Year C—Luke
- Where Is Your Heart?—Luke 12:32-40
- Parable of Shrewd Manager—Luke 16:1-13

Discuss:
- How we treat the world and our possessions says volumes about how we feel about God. Reflect on how well you take care of the people and the environment around you. How do they concern you?
- Describe a time when you gave away something you treasured. What feelings did you have at the time? What is the passion of your heart?

Closing

Close with the Lord's Prayer or another favorite prayer.

Session 5:
Seek and Serve

PLAN THE SESSION

Celebrant: Will you seek and serve Christ in all persons, loving your neighbor as yourself?

People: I will, with God's help.

To Bring

- 2 Bibles
- 2 copies of *The Book of Common Prayer*

Optional:
- information about parish or community ministries

Matters of Time and Place

How much time you spend on each session can be flexible, depending on what you and the confirmand you will be mentoring have available, but aim for between 45 minutes and an hour and a half. Choose a meeting place that will be comfortable for both of you: a quiet room at church, the student's home, your home, a coffee shop, or even somewhere outside if weather permits.

The Session at a Glance

- Welcome the student you are mentoring. Do a check-in to see how you both have been faring since your previous session.

- Pray the appropriate vow from the Baptismal Covenant responsively.
- Share questions and conversation.
- Close with prayer.

Before the Session

- Select a meeting place.
- Extend an e-mail or phone invitation to the confirmand you're mentoring.
- Have two copies of *The Book of Common Prayer* and two Bibles in hand.
- Read through the suggested scripture passages and the questions for conversation; note your own responses to the questions.
- *Optional: gather information on local ministries.*

THE SESSION

Gather

Welcome the student you are accompanying as mentor on his or her journey of faith. Take time to check in with each other about any important events, experiences or ideas you have encountered since you last met.

To initiate this session, turn to page 305 in *The Book of Common Prayer* and pray the appropriate vow from the Baptismal Covenant, with the student as *Celebrant* and you as *People*.

For each of the following "Focus" segments, read the selected scripture passages and consider the questions for conversation.

Focus: Seek Your Neighbor

The Parable of the Good Samaritan—Luke 10:25-37
- Who are the Samaritans in our lives?
- How have you been the Good Samaritan to someone else?

Focus: Love Our Enemies

Year A—Matthew
- Matthew 5:43-48

Year B/C—Luke
- Luke 6:27-45

Discuss:
- Has there been a time when you have "turned the other cheek?"
- Why do you think Jesus encourages us to love our enemies?

Focus: The Great Commandment

Year A—Matthew
- Matthew 5:38-48
- Matthew 7:12
- Matthew 22:31-34

Year B/C—Mark
- Mark 12:28-34

Discuss:
- To live in a "perfect" way, God's love must flow through our lives to others, even to our enemies. To live the Golden Rule is to do to others as you would have them do to you. In the past few months, how have you fulfilled the Great Commandment?

- Why is it so difficult for us to love our neighbors?
- How is it different to love our enemies?
- Why is it sometimes impossible to love ourselves?

Focus: Who Are the Unlovable?

Year A—Matthew
- Matthew 9:9-13
  — Why was Matthew hated?

Year B—Mark
- Mark 2:13-17
  — Why was Levi (another name for Matthew, the tax collector) despised? (See Glossary, p. 41, for more information.)

Year C—Luke
- Luke 19:1-10
  — Why was Zacchaeus disliked? How was Zacchaeus saved?

The Mission of the Church—to restore *all* people to unity of God
- *The Book of Common Prayer*, page 855).

Discuss:
- What is it that Jesus wants from others/us?

Focus: To Serve—The Kingdom Spreads

Year A—Matthew
- Parable of the Mustard Seed and the Yeast— Matthew 13:31-33
- Parable of the Ten Virgins—Matthew 25:1-13
- Parable of the Three Servants—Matthew 25:14-30
- Parable of the Faithful Servant—Matthew 24:45-51

- Coming of the Kingdom—Matthew 24:23-28,36-44

Year B—Mark
- Parable of the Mustard Seed—Mark 4:26-34
- For/Against—Mark 9:38-41
- Teaching of Ancestors—Mark 7:1-13
- Pharisees—Mark 8:14-21

Year C—Luke
- Parable of the Mustard Seed and the Yeast— Luke 13:18-21
- Parable of the Watchful Servant—Luke 12:35-40
- Parable of the Faithful Servant—Luke 12:41-48
- Coming of the Kingdom—Luke 17:20-37

Discuss:
- To serve is to give of one's time without payment or remuneration of any kind.
- Have you ever done something for someone else without anyone knowing about it? What was it like?

We Are Given the Great Commission— Matthew 25:31-46
- How can we choose to further the Kingdom?
- Is there a ministry in your parish and/or your community in which you can make a difference?

Optional: share information about some parish or community ministries.

Closing

Close with the Lord's Prayer, the St. Francis Prayer (*BCP* p. 833) or another favorite prayer.

Session 6: Into the World in Witness

PLAN THE SESSION

Celebrant: Will you strive for justice and peace among all people, and respect the dignity of every human being?

People: I will, with God's help.

To Bring

- 2 Bibles
- 2 copies of *The Book of Common Prayer*

Optional:

- brochures or printouts about various outreach/social justice organizations
- a card, bookmark or other small token of gratitude for being invited to share this part of your confirmand's spiritual journey

Matters of Time and Place

Since this is the last planned session, you should by now have a pretty good idea of how much time to allow within the 45-90 minute framework.

Choose a familiar meeting place—or a special one for this final planned session.

Consider other opportunities to spend time with this student, before and/or after Confirmation, perhaps going to a museum or a movie...or simply taking a walk together.

The Session at a Glance

- Welcome the student you are mentoring; do a check-in to see how you both have been faring since your previous Session.
- Pray the appropriate vow from the Baptismal Covenant responsively.
- Share questions and conversation.
- Close with prayer.

Before the Session

- Select a meeting place.
- Extend an email or phone invitation to the confirmand you're mentoring.
- Have two copies of *The Book of Common Prayer* and two Bibles in hand.
- Read through the suggested scripture passages and the questions for conversation; note your own responses to the questions.
- *Optional: collect brochures or printouts about various outreach/social justice organizations that might be of interest to your confirmand.*
- *Optional: acquire or make a card, bookmark, or other small token to honor the relationship you have built with the student you have been mentoring.*

THE SESSION

Gather

Welcome the student you have accompanied as mentor during this stage of his or her faith journey. Take time to check in with each other about any important events, experiences or ideas you have encountered since you last met.

Acknowledge your gratitude for being able to share this time of formation.

To initiate this session, turn to page 305 in *The Book of Common Prayer* and pray the appropriate vow from the Baptismal Covenant, with the student as *Celebrant* and you as *People*.

For each of the following "Focus" segments, read the selected scripture passages and consider the questions for conversation.

Authority/Permission

Year A—*Matthew*
- Jesus' Authority—Matthew 7:28-29; Matthew 12:15-32; Matthew 21:23-27
  — Where does Jesus get his authority?
- Peter's Declaration—Matthew 16:13-20
- Jesus' Baptism—Matthew 3:13-17
  — How does Jesus' baptism empower him to do his mission?
- Our Authority—Matthew 10:26-42; Matthew 21:33-46
  — Where do we get our authority?

Year B—Mark

- Jesus' Authority—Mark 6:1-6; Mark 11:20-33; Mark 12:35-40
  — Where does Jesus get his authority?
- Peter's Declaration—Mark 8:27-30
- Jesus' Baptism—Mark 1:9-13
  — How does Jesus' baptism empower him to do his mission?
- Eyes on God—Mark 12:13-17; Mark 14:3-11
  — How do we keep our eyes on God?
- Our Authority—Mark 1:14-20; Mark 2:23-28; Mark 3:13-19
  — Where do we get our authority?

Year C—Luke

- Jesus' Authority—Luke 11:14-23; Luke 20:1-8
  — Where does Jesus get his authority?
- Jesus' Baptism—Luke 3:21-22
  — How does Jesus' baptism empower him to do his mission?
- Our Authority—Luke 12:4-12; Luke 20:9-19
  — Where do we get our authority?

Discuss:

- How does our baptism empower us? (See "Holy Baptism," BCP p. 299.)
- Where is the Church empowered? (See "Mission of the Church," BCP p. 855.)

Mission of Peace and Justice

Year A—Matthew
- Justice—Matthew 25:36-46
  - Where is the message of justice in the world today?
- Jesus Cleansing the Temple—Matthew 21:12-17
  - Why does Jesus cleanse the Temple?

Year B—Mark
- Justice—Matthew 25:36-46
  - Where is the message of Justice in the world today?
- Jesus Cleansing the Temple—Mark 11:15-19
  - Why does Jesus cleanse the Temple?

Year C—Luke
- Justice—Luke 17:20-37
  - Where is the message of Justice in the world today?
- Jesus Cleansing the Temple—Luke 19:28-47
  - Why does Jesus cleanse the Temple?

Discuss:
- Do we get angry when we see others "cheated" or mistreated?

Dignity of Every Human Being

Year A—Matthew
- Widows—Luke 18:1-8
- Children—Matthew 19:13-15
- Tax Collectors—Matthew 19:16-30
- Lepers—Luke 17:11-19
- All Are Precious in the Sight of God—Matthew 7:7-11

Year B—Mark
- Widows—Mark 12:37-40
- Children—Mark 10:13-16

- Tax Collectors—Mark 2:13-17
- Lepers—Luke 17:11-19
- All Are Precious in the Sight of God—Luke 11:9-13

Year C—Luke
- Widows—Luke 18:1-8
- Children—Luke 18:15-17
- Tax Collectors—Luke 18:9-30
- Lepers—Luke 17:11-19
- All are precious in the sight of God—Luke 11:9-13

Discuss:
- Who are the outcasts today?
- Where are the injustices in your life?
- Where can we bring peace and justice in our corner of the world?

Sending Forth

Year A—Matthew
- Parable of the Talents—Matthew 25:14-30
- Mission and Cost of Discipleship—Matthew 10:5-24
- Sending in Pairs—Luke 10:1-12

Year B—Mark
- Parable of the Talents—Luke 19:11-27
- Mission and Cost of Discipleship—Mark 13:1-13; Mark 6:14-29
- Sending in Pairs—Luke 10:1-12

Year C—Luke
- Parable of the Talents—Luke 19:11-27
- Cost of Discipleship—Luke 14:25-35
- Sending in Pairs—Luke 10:1-12

Discuss:
- How is ministry more effective in numbers?
- What outreach ministry could you get passionate about?
- How are we furthering the Kingdom?
- How are we using our talents/resources to help others?

Optional: share brochures and printouts about outreach and social justice organizations.

Optional: give a card or other reminder of this shared time with your student.

Closing

Close with the Lord's Prayer, another favorite prayer or the "General Thanksgiving" on page 836 in *The Book of Common Prayer.*

Glossary

from *Young Reader's Bible Dictionary*, Revised Edition,
Abingdon Press, 2000. Used by permission.

High Priest

Chief of the priests in the temple at Jerusalem. He acted as the
representative of the people before God. (See *Priests and Levites*.)
*Numbers 35:25,28; 2 Kings 22:4,8; Haggai 1:1,12,14; Matthew
26:57-66; Mark 14:53-54; John 11:49-52.*

Leprosy (LEP-ruh-see)

A serious skin disease. In Bible times persons who had leprosy
were forced to live apart from others. They were considered reli-
giously unclean. The term "leprosy" in Bible times was probably
used for many types of skin diseases. The priest had to observed
the skin disease and determine whether or not it was leprosy.
Today leprosy is often called Hansen's disease, and some forms
are curable. *Leviticus 13:1-14:54; Numbers 5:2 2 Kings 5:1-27; 2
Chronicles 26:19-21; Matthew 8:2-4; 10:8; Mark 1:40-44; Luke
5:12-15; 17:11-19.*

Pharisees (FAIR-uh-seez)

A powerful religious party among the Jews in NT times. These
men were not priests but laymen who were trained in the law.
Their belief in the resurrection after death and their strict way
of following the law made them different from the Sadducees,
another religious party (see *Sadducees*). The Pharisees expected
the royal line of David to be restored and with it the politi-
cal power of Jerusalem and Israel. The Pharisees opposed Jesus
because he did not insist on keeping the law as strictly as they
did, and because he did not keep away from sinners. Paul, who

became an apostle after the Resurrection, was a member of the Pharisees. After he became a Christian, he saw that the law of love as taught by Jesus was more important than the strict law of the Pharisees. This party continued to oppose Christians and the early church throughout NT times. *Matthew 9:11-13; 12:2-8; 22:15-22; Mark 2:16-17; Luke 11:37-44, 53; John 11:46-48, 57; 18:3-6; Acts 15:5; 23:6-9.*

Priests and Levites (preests, LEE-vites)

Those who stand before God as his servants. Under the covenant of Moses the whole nation of Israel was to be a "kingdom of priests." They were to be a holy people fit to serve God. Their holiness proved to be very imperfect in actual practice. However, the idea of holiness was symbolized in the official priesthood. Among the Israelites the priesthood developed into three divisions—high priest, priest, and Levite, each having its own distinctive functions and privileges. The high priest represented all the people of Israel before God in the sanctuary. He alone could enter the holy of holies once a year to make atonement for the nation's sin. The priests took care of the sanctuary, taught the law, and took part in the sacrifices. The Levites assisted the priests and were responsible for the care of the temple, cleaning the sacred vessels, preparing the cereal offering, and carrying out the service of praise. They represented the people of Israel as substitutes for the firstborn sons who belonged, by right, to God. In the OT the priesthood began with Moses. He consecrated his brother Aaron and Aaron's sons to be priests. These men were of the tribe of Levi, the traditional priestly tribe.* *Exodus 19:6; 28:1,40-43; I Samuel 1:9; 5:5; I Chronicles 15:14; 2 Chronicles 34:14; Ezra 3:2; Nehemiah 3:1; Luke 1:5; Acts 4:1,6; Hebrews 7:23-24; I Peter 2:9.*

*Author's note: all priests were Levites, but not all Levites were priests.

Sadducees (SAJ-eh-seez)

In NT times a priestly religious party of the Jews. The high priest in the temple was chosen from among this group. Well educated and aristocratic, the Sadducees were in the majority in the high council in Jerusalem. The big difference between the Sadducees and the Pharisees, another religious party, was in their interpretation of the law. The Sadducees differed with the Pharisees over the question of the resurrection of the dead (see *Pharisees*). The Sadducees did not believe in the resurrection of the dead, probably because it was not found in the law. Jesus told them they were wrong and that they did not understand the scriptures or the power of God. *Matthew 3:7; 16:1-12; 22:23; Mark 12:18-27; Luke 20:27-40; Acts 4:1-2; 5:17; 23:6-10.*

Samaritans (suh-MAIR-i-tuhnz)

The mixed peoples of Samaria. Many of them did not follow the law and worship of the Hebrews. The Samaritans established their center for worship on Mt. Gerizim rather than at Jerusalem. The Jews who returned to Judah from their exile in Babylon found the leaders in Samaria against the rebuilding of Jerusalem and the temple. This was one of the causes of the ill feeling that existed between the Jews and Samaritans in NT times. *2 Kings 17:29; Matthew 10:5; Luke 9:52; 17:16; John 4:2-42; Acts 8:25.*

Sanhedrin (san-HE-drin)

The supreme Jewish council in Jerusalem following the Exile. It was presided over by the high priest and consisted of seventy-one members chosen from among the priests, scribes, Sadducees, and Pharisees. The Sanhedrin had the authority to make laws for the Jews and to judge lawbreakers. Jesus, Peter, John, Stephen, and Paul appeared before this council. *Matthew 26:59; Mark 14:55-63; 15:1; Luke 22:6; John 11:47-53; Acts 4:13-20; 5:17-29; 6:8-15; 22:30; 24:20.*

Scribe

Originally a person who could write. The scribe was important to a king because he could write messages and keep records. OT scribes became a professional class of men during the Exile. They studied, interpreted, and taught the Jewish law. They came from the families of priests and were probably responsible for gathering together and setting down many of Israel's sacred writings, which make up the OT of today. NT scribes were a professional group defending and teaching the law. They were important in the Sanhedrin, which was the high council in Jerusalem. Some were members of a religious party called the Pharisees. *1 Chronicles 27:32; 2 Chronicles 34:13; Ezra 4:8-10; 7:6, 11-12, 21; Nehemiah 8:1,4,9,13; 12:26, 36; Psalm 45:1; Jeremiah 8:8; 36:32; Matthew 2:4; 8:19; 13:52; Mark 2:6, 16; 7:1; Luke 20:1, 19; Acts 6:12; 23:9.*

Tax Collector, Tax Office

An official who collects and keeps account of taxes; the table or booth set up at the gate of the city, on a caravan route, or in the marketplace for collecting taxes. Tax collectors are never popular, and to the Jews of NT times they were especially despised because they represented the foreign authority of Rome. Very often these revenue officers charged too much in order to keep some part of the money for themselves. *Matthew 9:9-11; 11:19; 18:17; Mark 2:14-16; Luke 5:27-30.*

Zacchaeus (zuh-KEE-uhss)

Chief tax collector of Jericho. The life of this man was changed when he met and taLukeed with Jesus. *Luke 19:1-10.*

Appendix 1: Map of Israel at Time of Jesus

Appendix 2: The Bible and The Book of Common Prayer

The Bible is a collection of individual books, which Christians divide into the Old Testament and the New Testament. The Old Testament, first written in Hebrew, begins with Creation and follows the history of the Hebrew people. The New Testament, first written in Greek, begins with the life and teachings of Jesus and includes documents from the early Church. The Old Testament is sometimes referred to as Hebrew Scripture in acknowledgement of its origins; the New Testament is sometimes referred to as Greek Scripture because of its original language. The Dead Sea Scrolls contain the most ancient copies of Old Testament writings. The Septuagint is the oldest known Greek translation of the entire Old Testament; it contains additional books called the Apocrypha, which means "hidden" and is sometimes interpreted to mean "writings hidden for safekeeping." (Because not all biblical scholars agree on the canonical status of these books, not all versions of the Bible include the Apocrypha.) The New Testament contains four gospels ("gospel" means "good news"): Matthew, Mark, Luke and John. These are followed by the Acts of the Apostles, which tells the history of the early Church, and then the epistles (or letters), and finally the Book of Revelation. The Bible includes history, wisdom, poetry, prophesies, visions and stories to help us know the face of God, and it says much about the relationship between God and humankind.

During the time of the Roman Empire, when Latin replaced Greek as the dominant language, the scriptures were translated into Latin. In 1611 under King James (and the Church of England) the Bible was translated from Hebrew and Greek into English. The King James Bible is an eloquent translation, which for over three hundred years was the dominant English version. During the 1950's, the scriptures were translated into English using more contemporary vocabulary. Now we have many translations from which to choose; some include the Apocrypha, while others do not.

To find a passage in the Bible, look up the name of the book in the table of contents. The first number following the name of the book is the chapter of the text. The numbers following the colon are the verses. For example, Luke 2:1-12 is the second chapter of the book of Luke, beginning at the first verse and ending with the twelfth verse.

In the Episcopal Church, we follow a three-year lectionary, or cycle of scripture readings, in our worship. Each week there is a "proper" which contains four passages: usually an Old Testament reading, a psalm, a selection from an epistle or other New Testament reading, and a gospel reading. In year A, the gospel readings are primarily drawn from Matthew. During Year B, the primary gospel is Mark, and in year C it is Luke. The Gospel of John is interspersed throughout the three years. The scripture readings are preceded by an opening prayer known as the "collect," which often includes thematic references to one or more of the readings.

The Book of Common Prayer (BCP) is our primary book of worship, uniting us in common prayer. About 80% of the prayer book incorporates language from scripture; it includes many different services for various worship and pastoral purposes throughout the Church seasons. The new Church year begins with Advent.

Besides the more familiar Eucharist and daily offices, the *BCP* includes the entire book of Psalms, prayers for the home (pp. 814-839), the Catechism (pp. 845-862), and much more. The first Anglican prayer book, dating back to 1549, was written under the initiative of Thomas Cranmer for the Church of England. *The Book of Common Prayer* that we currently use in the Episcopal Church was published in the United States in 1979. Under the previous 1928 *Book of Common Prayer*, no one was allowed to receive Communion until after being confirmed. The 1979 prayer book restored the early Church practice of including the newly baptized at the Eucharist. Although each new revision of the prayer book contains changes that are both theological and stylistic, *The Book of Common Prayer* continues to bind us together in worship and prayer.

For more reading, see *Opening the Bible* by Roger Ferlo and *Opening the Prayer Book* by Jeffrey D. Lee, from *The New Church's Teaching Series* (Cowley Publications).

Appendix 3: The Gospel of Matthew (Year A)

Background on the Gospel of Matthew

Here's what we know about the Gospel of Matthew:

- Written about 90 A.D.
- Written from a Jewish perspective and probably addressed to Jewish converts.
- Jesus chose 12 of his many disciples (learners who followed Jesus) to be his "apostles"—those sent to be teachers.
- Matthew is sometimes called Levi. He was a tax collector, despised because he was seen as helping the Romans oppress the Jews.
- Matthew begins with a genealogy of Jesus and quotes the Hebrew prophecies of old to show the relationship between Jesus and God's ancient promises to the Jewish people.
- Matthew addresses the growing sense that Christ's return in glory was not likely to happen as quickly as first thought.
- This gospel is a manual of Christian teachings, administration, discipline and worship that responds to the question of how Christians should live in the meantime.

- Matthew is unique in organizing Jesus' teaching into five discourses, including the Sermon on the Mount (chapters 5-7), the longest single piece of Jesus' teaching in the Bible.
- The Gospel of Matthew seems to be patterned after the Torah with the five discourses to match the five Deuteronomic books, for example, the flight into Egypt echoes the Hebrew Egyptian captivity, and Jesus' Sermon on the Mount parallels the giving of the Mosaic law on Mount Sinai.

(Adapted from Grenz, Linda L. *Pocket Bible Guide*. New York: Doubleday, 1997. Used by permission.)

Outline of the Gospel of Matthew

- Matthew 1:1-17—Genealogy of the Messiah
- Matthew 1:18–2:23—Birth of Jesus & flight into Egypt
- Matthew 3—Jesus' Baptism
- Matthew 4:1-11—Temptations
- Matthew 4:12-28—Beginning of public ministry and calling of Disciples
- Matthew 5–7—The Five Discourses
  - First Discourse—Sermon on the Mount: Matthew 5:1–7:29 (including the Beatitudes: 5:3-11, the Lord's Prayer: 6:9-13 and the Golden Rule: 7:12)
  - Second Discourse—Matthew 10: Commissioning of the Twelve (Missions)
  - Third Discourse—Matthew 13: Kingdom Parables
  - Fourth Discourse—Matthew 18: Church Discipline
  - Fifth Discourse—Matthew 24–25: Destruction of Temple, Signs, Warnings (Eschatology)
- Matthew 26–27—Trial and Crucifixion
- Matthew 28—Resurrection Appearances and the Disciples' "Great Commission"

The Gospel of Matthew in 30 Days

1. Birth of Christ—Matthew (Matt) 1:1-25
2. Wise Men and Flight into Egypt—Matthew 2:1-23
3. John the Baptist and Jesus' Baptism—Matthew 3:1-17
4. Temptations—Matthew 4:1-11
5. Ministry and Calling Disciples—Matthew 4:12-25
6. Sermon on the Mount—Matthew 5:1-48
7. Teachings—Matthew 6:1-34
8. Seek and Find—Matthew 7:1-29
9. Healings—Matthew 8:1-34
10. More Healings—Matthew 9:1-38
11. Mission of Apostles—Matthew 10:1-42
12. Come to Me—Matthew 11:1-30
13. Keeping the Sabbath—Matthew 12:1-50
14. Parables—Matthew 13:1-58
15. Miracles—Matthew 14:1-36
16. Have Faith—Matthew 15:1-39
17. Peter's Declaration—Matthew 16:1-28
18. Transfiguration—Matthew 17:1-27
19. Lost Sheep—Matthew 18:1-35
20. Divorce, Children and Young Rich Man—Matthew 19:1-30
21. The Vineyard—Matthew 20:1-34
22. Entry into Jerusalem—Matthew 21:1-46
23. Wedding Feast and Great Commandment—Matthew 22:1-46
24. Signs and Warnings—Matthew 23:1-39
25. Faithful Servant—Matthew 24:1-51
26. Parables and Final Judgment—Matthew 25:1-46
27. Last Supper—Matthew 26:1-30
28. Arrest of Jesus—Matthew 26:31-75
29. Trial and Crucifixion—Matthew 27:1-66
30. Resurrection and Great Commission—Matthew 28:1-20

Appendix 4:
The Gospel of Mark
(Year B)

Background on the Gospel of Mark

The Gospel of Mark can be read in one sitting. It's interesting to read it like a "novel"—one seems to get the humor and personality of Jesus in a different way than from hearing the snippets in the Sunday lectionary.

Here's what we know about the Gospel of Mark:

- It is the shortest and oldest gospel (manuscript "R" for original source.)
- Often read as introductory overview of the story of Jesus.
- Written for Gentiles (Matthew written for Jews) during Christian persecution under Emperor Nero.
- Probably written after the destruction of the Temple* in Jerusalem in 70 A.D.
- Begins with the "Good News" about Jesus Christ, Son of God.
- Begins with Baptism of Jesus—his point of public ministry.
- Jesus is pictured as man of action and authority:
  — teaching
  — healing; demonstrating power over evil
  — working miracles
  — forgiving people's sins

- Mark stresses Jesus' suffering and death with implications that Jesus' followers will also embrace self-sacrificial service.
- Mark offers two ending. The first ends at 16:9-10; the other ends with verses 9-20 and may have been added later or brought in from another manuscript. The original ending may be lost.
- Mark encourages readers to remain faithful in times of trouble.

(Adapted from Grenz, Linda L. *Pocket Bible Guide*. New York: Doubleday, 1997. Used by permission.)

*There were two Temples built on the same site: one built by King Solomon and destroyed in 586 BCE, and one built by Zerubbabel after the Exile, completed about 515 BCE with expansion/restoration under Herod around 20 BCE. This second Temple was destroyed in 70 CE. The Muslim Dome of the Rock now sits on this site. The Western Wall of the Temple is still accessible in Jerusalem as a sacred site for Jews and Christians alike.

Outline of the Gospel of Mark

- Mark 1–3—Proclamation of the Kingdom of God
- Mark 4:1-34—Parables of the Kingdom of God
- Mark 4:35–8:26—Miracles
- Mark 8:27–10:52—Discipleship
- Mark 11–13—Last Week in Jerusalem
- Mark 14–15—Trial and Crucifixion
- Mark 16—The Empty Tomb and the Risen Lord

The Gospel of Mark in 30 Days

1. John the Baptist and Jesus' Baptism—Mark 1:1-20
2. Jesus begins Ministry and Preaching—Mark 1:21-45
3. Ministry and Calling First Disciples—Mark 2:1-17
4. Questions of Fasting and Sabbath—Mark 2:18-28
5. Ministry and Calling 12 Apostles—Mark 3:1-35
6. Parables—Mark 4:1-34
7. Miracle of Walking on Water—Mark 4:35-41
8. Healings—Mark 5:1-42
9. Jesus Rejected and Sending Disciples—Mark 6:1-12
10. Death of John the Baptist—Mark 6:14-29
11. Miracles and Healing—Mark 6:30-56
12. Teachings—Mark 7:1-23
13. Have Faith—Mark 7:24-37
14. More Miracles—Mark 8:1-26
15. Peter's Declaration—Mark 8:27-9:1
16. Transfiguration—Mark 9:2-29
17. Jesus' End Is Near—Mark 9:30-50
18. Divorce, Children and the Rich Man—Mark 10:1-31
19. Jesus' Time Is Near and Bartimaeus—Mark 10:32-52
20. Entry into Jerusalem—Mark 11:1-11
21. Signs and Warnings—Mark 11:12-33
22. Parable of the Vineyard and More—Mark 12:1-27
23. The Great Commandment—Mark 12:28-34
24. Trouble and Persecution—Mark 12:35–13:23
25. Coming of the Son of Man—Mark 13:24–14:2
26. Anointing at Bethany—Mark 14:3-9
27. Last Supper—Mark 14:10-42
28. Arrest and Trial—Mark 14:43–15:15
29. Crucifixion and Burial—Mark 15:16-47
30. Resurrection and Ascension—Mark 16:1–end

Appendix 5: The Gospel of Luke (Year C)

Background on the Gospel of Luke

Here's what we know about the Gospel of Luke:

- Luke's is the longest of the gospels.
- Luke is the first part of a work that is continued in the book of the Acts (of the Apostles).
- It was written about 90 A.D., most likely by and for Gentile Christians.
- Luke, whom tradition identifies as a physician, worked with Paul.
- He gathered accounts from people who knew Jesus and carefully arranged them so they would tell the story in a logical progression.
- Luke presents Jesus both as the culmination of God's promises to the Hebrew people and as a universal savior.
- Through the stories of Jesus he selects, Luke demonstrates special concern for prayer, the Holy Spirit, the outcast and the role of women in the church.

(Adapted from Grenz, Linda L. *Pocket Bible Guide*. New York: Doubleday, 1997. Used by permission.)

Outline for the Gospel of Luke

- Luke 1–2—Birth of John and Jesus; Jesus' Childhood
- Luke 3—John Baptizes Jesus
- Luke 4–6—Jesus in Galilee
- Luke 7–8—Miracles and Parables
- Luke 9—Jesus and the Twelve
- Luke 9:51–11:13—To Jerusalem
- Luke 11:14–14:35—Opposition (from established religious leaders, for example, the Pharisees)
- Luke 15—Parables of the Lost Sheep, the Lost Coin and the Prodigal Son
- Luke 16–18—Instruction to Disciples
- Luke 18:31–19:48—Jesus Begins Journey to Jerusalem (for Passover)
- Luke 21—Last Week in Jerusalem; Warnings and Signs
- Luke 22—Last Supper
- Luke 22:47–23:56—Trial and Crucifixion
- Luke 24—Resurrection and Post-Resurrection Stories

The Gospel of Luke in 30 Days

1. Announcement of Jesus' birth—Luke 1:1-38.
2. Praise and Prophecy—Luke 1:39-80
3. Birth of Jesus—Luke 2:1-38
4. Boy Jesus—Luke 2:39-52
5. John the Baptist, Baptism and Genealogy—Luke 3:1-38
6. Temptation—4:1-13
7. Beginning of Ministry—Luke 4:14-44
8. Call of Disciples—Luke 5:1-39
9. Teachings—Luke 6:1-26
10. Loving Enemies and Judging Others—Luke 6:27-49
11. Healings—Luke 7:1-50
12. Parables and Miracles—Luke 8:1-56

13. Sending Out and Feeding 5000—Luke 9:1-28
14. Transfiguration—Luke 9:29-62
15. Parable of Good Samaritan—Luke 10:1-41
16. Lord's Prayer—Luke 11:1-53
17. Parables of Watchfulness—Luke 12:1-59
18. Parables of Growth—Luke 13:1-35
19. Cost of Discipleship—Luke 14:1-34
20. Parables of Lost and Found—Luke 15:1-32
21. Shrewd Sayings—Luke 16:1-31
22. Coming of the Kingdom—Luke 17:1-37
23. Blessings and Healings—Luke 18:1-43
24. Zacchaeus and Palm Sunday—Luke 19:1-47
25. Questioning Authority—Luke 20:1-47
26. Warnings and Destruction—Luke 21:1-38
27. Last Supper—Luke 22:1-62
28. Trial—Luke 22:63–23:25
29. Crucifixion and Resurrection—Luke 23:26–24:12
30. Post Resurrection Sightings—Luke 24:13-53

Bibliography

Augustine, Peg. *Young Reader's Bible Dictionary, Revised Edition*. Nashville: Abingdon Press, 2000.

Grenz, Linda L. *Pocket Bible Guide*. New York: Doubleday, 1997.

Taylor, Barbara Brown. *The Preaching Life*. Cowley Publications, 1993.

Wile, Mary Lee. *I will, with God's Help*. Denver: Morehouse Education Resources, 2000.

Young, Francis M. *The Making of the Creeds*. London: SCM Press, 1991.My Spiritual Journey

Notes

. . . .

. . . .

. . . .

. . . .

. . . .

. . . .

. . . .

. . . .

. . . .

. . . .

. . . .

. . . .

. . . .

. . . .

. . . .

. . . .

. . . .

. . . .

. . . .

. . . .

. . . .

. . . .

. . . .

. . . .

. . . .

. . . .

. . . .

I will, with God's help